Dear Parent:

Your child's love of re

Every child learns to read in a diff⟶ ⟶ ⟶speed. Some go back and forth between reading levels and read favorite books again and again. Others read through each level in order. You can help your young reader improve and become more confident by encouraging his or her own interests and abilities. From books your child reads with you to the first books he or she reads alone, there are I Can Read Books for every stage of reading:

SHARED READING
Basic language, word repetition, and whimsical illustrations, ideal for sharing with your emergent reader

BEGINNING READING
Short sentences, familiar words, and simple concepts for children eager to read on their own

READING WITH HELP
Engaging stories, longer sentences, and language play for developing readers

READING ALONE
Complex plots, challenging vocabulary, and high-interest topics for the independent reader

I Can Read Books have introduced children to the joy of reading since 1957. Featuring award-winning authors and illustrators and a fabulous cast of beloved characters, I Can Read Books set the standard for beginning readers.

A lifetime of discovery begins with the magical words **"I Can Read!"**

Visit www.icanread.com for information
on enriching your child's reading experience.

Visit www.zonderkidz.com for more Zonderkidz I Can Read! titles.

All the people saw it. Then they fell down flat with their faces toward the ground. They cried out, "The Lord is the one and only God! The Lord is the one and only God!"

1 Kings 18:39

ZONDERKIDZ

Elijah, God's Mighty Prophet
Copyright © 2016 by Zondervan
Illustrations © 2016 by David Miles

Requests for information should be addressed to:
Zonderkidz, 3900 Sparks Drive SE, Grand Rapids, Michigan 49546

ISBN 978-0-310-75081-9

Editor: Mary Hassinger
Art direction and design: Kris Nelson

Printed in China

22 23 24 /DSC / 20 19 18 17 16 15 14 13 12 11 10 9 8 7 6

Adventure BIBLE

Elijah, God's Mighty Prophet

Pictures by David Miles

ZONDERkidz

Elijah lived in Israel,

the Promised Land

that God gave to the Jews.

Elijah was a prophet.

He was a messenger from God.

But people didn't always listen.

At that time, Ahab, the king,

did not pray to the true God.

He prayed to a god called Baal.

So did many other Jews.

Elijah made an announcement.

He said, "There will be no more rain

in Israel until I say so.

God is not happy with you."

What Elijah said came true.

The streams dried up.

Plants could not grow.

People were hungry and thirsty.

But God took care of Elijah.

God showed Elijah a stream.

God sent ravens

to bring Elijah bread and meat.

One day, Elijah saw a woman

gathering sticks.

He asked,

"Would you bring me some bread?"

The woman said, "I have no bread.

I only have a little flour and oil.

When that is gone,

my son and I will die."

11

Elijah told the woman,

"Go home and bake some bread.

You will not run out of flour or oil."

The woman did as Elijah said.

No matter how much oil or flour she used,

the woman did not run out.

God provided food for Elijah,

the woman, and her son.

But King Ahab was very angry.

He wanted Elijah to make it rain again.

God told Elijah

to go meet King Ahab.

When Ahab saw Elijah, he said,

"You have brought trouble!"

Elijah said,

"You have caused the trouble.

You pray to Baal.

You do not pray to the true God."

Then Elijah said,

"Call all the prophets of Baal

and all the people of Israel.

Have them meet me on Mount Carmel."

Elijah stood before the people.

He said, "How long

will you go back and forth?

If the Lord is God, follow him.

But if Baal is god, follow him."

The people said nothing.

Then Elijah said,

"Let's see who the real God is!

Let's have a contest!"

19

Elijah said,

"Let's put wood on two altars.

One altar is for your god, Baal.

The other altar is for my God."

"We will each call on our god.

The god who sends fire to the wood

is the true God."

The people liked this idea.

The prophets of Baal went first.

They put a bull on their altar.

They danced around

and shouted the name of Baal

from morning to noon.

In the afternoon, Elijah said,

"Maybe your god is sleeping.

Maybe he is busy.

Shout louder!"

So the prophets of Baal shouted louder.

The prophets of Baal shouted all day,
but no one answered.
Then Elijah said to the people,
"Come with me."

Elijah stood before the Lord's altar,

which had been torn down.

He used twelve stones to fix it.

He put wood and a bull on it.

He dug a trench around it.

Then Elijah told some men,

"Pour four jars of water on the wood."

They poured water on the altar.

Elijah said, "Do it two more times."

Soon the wood was very wet.

Water ran down the altar

and even filled the trench.

Everyone wondered

how the altar would burn.

Elijah stepped forward and prayed.

He said, "Lord, you are the true God,

and I am your servant.

Answer me so everyone will know

who you are!"

Fire came down from heaven!

It burned up the wood and the stones.

It burned up the bull and the soil.

It even dried the water in the trench!

When the people saw this,

they fell to their knees.

The people cried,

"The Lord is God!"

Soon after that, God sent rain.

The people could grow food

and find water again.

People in Bible Times

Elijah

Elijah was a prophet. His job was to give the people of Israel God's messages. God gave him the power to do miracles to help the people know that the Lord was the one true God.

Life in Bible Times

What exactly was a prophet in Bible times?

A prophet was person who received messages directly from God and then relayed them to God's people. This person is called by God to do this job. Sometimes the messages are God promising his everlasting love and others might be warnings to repent or try harder to follow his Word.